THEY ARE ALL GONE NOW
. . . .*And So Are YOU*

for Joyce

4/21/88

i

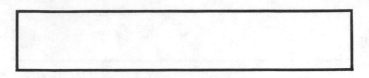

By the same author

A THIN BODY OF WORK
SUNFLOWERS
LET IT BE A DANCE
HIS & HERS
DRAGONFLIES, CODFISH & FROGS
(formerly Speaking Poems)
THE VOICE OF THE HIVE
STARK NAKED
EVEN AS WE SPEAK
DESERTED ROOSTER

They Are All Gone Now
~and so are YOU

by
Ric Masten

SUNFLOWER INK
Palo Colorado Canyon
Carmel, Calif. 93929

ACKNOWLEDGMENTS

Cover painting by Millard Sheets

**CLACK &
NICHOLS**
A PARTNERSHIP

THEY ARE ALL GONE NOW-*and so are* YOU produced by Clack & Nichols, A Partnership, 522 North Grant, Odessa, Texas 79761 Telephone number (915) 337-8511

(paperback) 9 8 7 6 5 4 3 2 1

Library of Congress Catalogue Card No. 85-50303
ISBN 0-931104-15-7

For my mother
HILDRETH TAYLOR MASTEN HARE
(June 1906—March 1984)

v

CONTENTS

Foreward #1. by Rev. Carolyn Sheets Owne-Towle
#2. by Ted Balgooyn

1. MORE THAN A SHOVELFUL OF DUST

2. THEY ARE ALL GONE NOW AND SO ARE YOU

3. NOTES FOR A TROUBADOUR AND TRAVELING SALESMAN

4. SEVEN SONGS UNSUNG

5. BACKWORD by Paul Benson 87

#1

Ric Masten's poetry is tenacious. He burrows in on a subject exposing its essence. He has a way of irritating the shell of experience until the meaning runs out. By focusing his pen on a small life fragment he puts you in touch with universal human experience. To which, of course, your response is "ahhhh yes."

To illuminate his subjects the poet uses both ends of the telescope. He thrusts you backward and forward in time, often in the same poem. There is a zoom effect. First you see someone far away, then close up; in the moment, then ages ago. Ric looks at life from fascinating vantage points.

This communicator is a non-romantic. He would rather wink at life with a wry eye than wax poetic. Yet his poetry sings of life with gentle humor and irony. So often in his work you assume you're headed down one path only to be jolted when another leads you off at a right angle. He forces you to reserve judgment by surprising you with unexpected conclusions.

At times you will hear a brave coward with a

wish to "be found face down, an arrow in the back
...taking me completely by surprise." At others
you'll recognize a vulnerable boy who camouflages
his hurts by making you laugh. Consistently, you
listen to a genuine human being whose unusual
insight helps him grapple with life's meanings.

Rev. Carolyn Sheets Owen-Towle
San Diego, California.

#2

As a teacher of humanities and communication
studies I have used Ric Masten's poetry for many
years to help college students become more aware of
the significance of their own lives. In the process, I
have greatly enriched the quality of my own.

This year, I have had the good fortune of getting a
sneak preview of this new volume of Ric's latest
work. I can assure new readers of the extraordinary
possibility of meeting themselves as well as Ric as he
explores the intimate scenes of his life. For long-time
Masten readers, Ric's reflections on mortality may

have a surprising, somber tone. He leads us to strange places where familiar faces are fading, and the deep-felt issue is where to hold fast to memory and where to let go. For new readers and old, there is the pleasure of being swept along by the rhythm and melody of Ric's conversational style, of discovering the unexpected importance he gives the unimportant, and of laughing at the quick, bright flashes of Masten humor.

Ric is known for doing most of his writing in the summer, but when autumn gold begins to fall, he begins his seasonal migration across America with his summer crop of poetry harvested. Because, above all, Ric is a person to person poet. Many of us along his route have been marking our calendars for Ric's stop for nearly two decades. As the time for his appearance draws near we begin to look for his jaunty figure and listen for the sound of his cheery voice. When at last he appears in his bulky sweater carrying his bulky loose leaf binder filled with poetry, we know another kind of season of the year has come.

I hope that Ric's poetry will add to your pleasure and strengthen your courage to meet the future face to face. You may even find the strength and courage to put the bits and pieces of your life into this pattern called poetry.

When I was in the sixth grade, I won a five dollar gold piece for writing a poem about the Statue of Liberty. That was over fifty years ago, and I haven't written a poem since—not for publication at any rate. The fact that I reached the pinnacle of success at such a tender age may have no tragic significance, but it serves to remind me of how fragile our creative impulses are and how much we owe to the brave poets of this world.

I cannot find the poetic words to express my appreciation for the pleasure and inner strength I've found in Ric Masten's poetry; but believe me, it has been considerable and I hope it will be considerable for all who read these pages.

Ted Balgooyn
Professor of Humanities
& Communication Studies
San Jose State University

AUTHOR'S NOTE

Because the title of a book is usually a poetic expression of its basic concept, it is possible then, to know what the title should be even before the first word has been written. The same can be said about a particular poem, but because a book of poetry does not necessarily write itself around a particular theme, it is always difficult to know what to call a collection. If a poem is like a single book then what do we call the library?

What a person who writes "Speaking Poems" does is look through the material to find out what he's been talking to himself about lately. And doing this I discovered almost every poem in this volume had something to do with people, places, times and things that no longer exist. Once I had this firmly in mind a line leaped out of context from one of the poems announcing that: THEY ARE ALL GONE NOW, and so are YOU.

xiv

They Are All Gone Now
~and so are YOU

1.

MORE THAN
A SHOVELFUL OF DUST

TOTO
SOMETHING TELLS ME
THIS AIN'T KANSAS. . .

"___and the dogs dwindle down
   to a precious few.
   September___"

the seven-to-one theory
makes our old dog Grace
a hundred and twenty-six
she arrived on my birthday
fun fixed up in a ribbon
i was thirty-five
and we went for a run

and now on my fifty-third
i'm puppied again
this time though
no spontaneous jog
just me
looking from dog to dog
calculating
that when he is as old as she
my God i'm seventy!

i know
age is a state of mind
a point of view
and i don't mean to be depressing
but figured in terrier time
i'm already
three hundred and seventy two

and that Dorothy
is far enough over the rainbow
to know
i haven't got many more Totos to go

3

THE POET GOES INTO
THE ELEMENTARY SCHOOL

good Lord!
it just came to me—
my shoes are older than almost
everyone
in this building

COMING OF AGE

i will admit
the young waitress
did flirt outrageously

my guess is
i closely resemble her dad
or perhaps her uncle Sid
the one who is such a big tease

but animal magnetism?
pleeese!

give it up boys
cut the hot-cha-cha
elbow in the ribs
i have a mirror and a clear sense
of myself

oh—
if i could wound her with a poem
show her moments
when i've held an audience trembling
in my grip
then perhaps

then
i might be something other
than the "balding little fat guy
who left an enormous tip"

TIME WARP

when i assured them all
i'd return next June

the children cried:
"gone so long?

the elders sighed:
"back so soon?"

UPON SEEING A DIGITAL WATCH
FOR THE FIRST TIME

if i live to be eighty
then i was more than half-way there
when Buzzy Jr.
flew his brand new Seiko
across the street

he
with the read-out lit in liquid crystal
just a kid
and all that science on his wrist

me
mouth agape
with a pocket Ben
twisting at the end of a chain
suddenly obsolete

it's like Grandville Glover
seeing an airplane for the first time
petrified
as the diving Barnstormer
scattered the horses
and left the crowd screaming

the baffling moment
lodged irretrievably in his brain

Grandpa
pulling up lame
as the rest of the world
flew off in another direction

7

MICK JAGGER TURNS EIGHTY AND TALKS ABOUT OLD TIMES

i recall how old man Glover
would wait in the throat
of family gatherings
the slightest contact
setting him off
like a Mackabe gopher trap

hi grampa
was all it took
to put me squirming on the hook
of the Great Depression
a young man learns
to sit at the far end of the table
and cut out early
for a picture show

(In those days the feature attraction was always
accompanied by short subjects. I remember one
about a scientist who went looking for himself in a
Time Machine. It ended with the boy he had once
been, on a park bench, beside the old man he was
destined to be. Unwilling to make the connection,
they sat there, back to back like bookends while the
credits rolled.)

right here
i will have to admit
i'm not absolutely certain
this film ever existed
a lot of what i remember
didn't

but last Thanksgiving Day
while telling Walter
my young nephew
about the Hippies
and what life was like
in the Haight Ashbury
something
very definitely snapped shut

BEGINNING THE DEATH WATCH

(in December 1982–DENIAL)

mother
has spent most of her adult life
in California
but like elephants
well-to-do ladies
from Brookline Massachusetts
know exactly
where their bones should lie

"when i die
 pack me off to Mount Auburn
 don't just sack and scuttle me
 out here on the West Coast"

and there is something else
i've recently learned
about elephants
they prefer to face death alone

"no need to come home
 you know how your younger brother
 exaggerates"
                    this counterpoint to:
"she refuses to see us
 i think the radiation
 is killing her"

and what can you say to that?
long distance
except how bad you feel
not being there to help
hoping they won't suspect
how glad you are that you aren't

and following this
the guilt

but life is never easy
and what was once the size of a fist
shrunk to the size of a pea

and this medical miracle
puts me right back in line
behind
a trumpeting old packaderm
who loves the circus
too much
to ever give up her ivory

11

HILDRETH

(in July 1983-ANGER)

mother
if i were God in Heaven
who would you send
to spend eternity with me?

the cherub
in the photograph
crying—holding a doll by the foot

the tomboy
racing a motorcycle
golden hair flying

the flapper
smoking her cigarette
in a long ivory holder

the perfect mother
parading a line
of perfect children

the widow
lifting her veil
married again in four months

the globetrotter
home with souvenirs
and an addiction

the alcoholic
the recovering
alcoholic

the eccentric
trying to look Egyptian

12

but resembling
a Buick hood-ornament

the closeted recluse
watching Wimbledon
from a Queensize bed

and now
a timid old woman
all nose and chin

mother
here on the eve of your departure
i don't know who
to put on the elevator

i only know that after some debate
your sons
will send your ashes East
to Massachusetts
where you have always said
you wanted them to go

that is
until yesterday
when it was too late
to let you change your mind

LAST WORDS

(in March 1984–RESOLUTION)

"tell us Gertrude, what's the answer?"
and it is reported
that the wily old poet
spent her last breath whispering:
"what's the question?"

and being
the same kind of irrepressible exotic
i had expected as much from you
at least
i was looking for something
more quotable
than: "hurry along now
        or you'll miss your movie"
but when mamma's gone
a mamma's-boy is free
to rearrange reality
and end your story with a more
dramatic scene played earlier that day

the one in which you groaned
tugging feebly
at the cloth restraint that held you
in what you must have known
would be your death-bed
saying: "cut me loose Ricky
        cut me loose"
mother
in this as in all things involving you
i can now
remember what i want to remember
and forget what i need to forget

14

THE EXILE

1. The Situation

tidying up
after the requiem
mother shipped my father East
his ashes swept beneath
a corner of her family's
family stone

"New England
 is glorious in the Fall"
 she wept
"and he'll be with the Phinnys
 and the Pratts"

but half a century
two more husbands
and a ship's captain later
(it's difficult to imagine
 the breathless multitude awaiting
 her favors on the other side)
she changed her mind

and when the dust settled
it was not
in that illustrious cemetery
on the East Coast
but at the foot
of a California redwood
close enough to her offspring
to keep us all
talking to a ghost

in death

as well as life
she kept to her favorite aphorism
"out of sight—out of mind"

and like a pea
under forty-three mattresses
my father's situation
began to bother me

2. *Incident at Mount Auburn*

"but why?
  when so many would gladly die
  for the privilege of being buried
  with all this Boston money
  why
  would you want your father exhumed?"

the puzzled director
threw up his hands
as i held the man at finger point
backing from the room
like a bandit
making off with a strong-box

outside
slapping my thighs
to sound like galloping horses
i ran for the wagon
a hail of imaginary bullets
kicking up dirt
in the asphalt parking lot

a nonexistent posse in hot pursuit
we shot through the ornamental gates

high-tailing it out of there
a split second before closing time

in reality
the incident described
was business-like
and most undramatic
a simple matter
of goods and services
bought and sold

but in traffic
that goes anywhere near my father
i drive
a Flexible Flyer coaster
and am never more
than twelve years old

3. *Viewing the Ashes*

who knows what i expected
something that would blow
away in the wind
i suppose
not a box of sand
and shell fragments

although
if i were insect size
i'd walk this chalky dune
hands clasped behind—eyes downcast
sifting the bits and pieces
searching for a Chambered Nautilus
that wasn't broken

17

common sense telling me
i might as well be looking
on the moon

still
if such a thing should exist
i'll find it
and put it to my ear
picking up the conversation
where you left it

4. *Conclusion at Wildcat Cove*

once
the handsome house
that crowns the shelf of rock
at Wildcat Cove
was home

my father
set the Spanish tile himself
and built the garden wall
with stones
hauled up from the beach below

since then
the property has changed hands
so many times
i can only guess who stands
at the window looking down
wondering
what these trespassers
have buried in the sand

my brother and i
buccaneers again
return to a childhood playground
and at the base of a once familiar cliff
place
like pirate treasure
the small brass chest
where only we could find it

and even though
the eulogy began and ended
with the words: what if ?
something more
than a shovelful of dust
was finally put to rest

later
leaving the experience
i reach a place far enough away
to have some real perspective
and looking back
see where our footprints
cross
a section of the beach

and realize
for the very first time
in my life
that the line continues on
out of sight
in both directions

THE STORM OF '83

atmospheric upheaval
elements
wild enough to send Lear
back to his bolt-cloven tree
and mean
enough to close Highway 1
for a year

deluge—
pluvial downpour
wet enough to give
a latter-day Noah ideas
and bring the choppers in low
with Alpo
for the animals we left behind

oh
i suppose
in strictly scientific terms
it will be regarded
only
as an interesting moment
in meteorological history

but happening in my yard
in my lifetime
it was a disaster!
the kind of event
grandfathers
have already
begun to exaggerate about

THE BUSINESS OF DYING

in my twenties
i went along with Dylan Thomas
boasting
that i wanted to die
looking death squarely in the eye

in my forties however
this brash statement
was somewhat revised
when i suddenly realized
that death wanted to come
and look me in the eye

nowadays
i find myself hoping
it happens
like it happens to the sentry
keeping guard
in all those Fort Apache movies

found dead—face down
an arrow in the back
"poor devil"
the Sergeant always said
"never knew what hit him"

i like that!

the end
taking me completely by surprise
the rest
left in the hands
of clever young writers
still wet behind the ears

WITH BIRTH
TO LOOK FORWARD TO

would it be easier
to live life in reverse
like a video-tape rewinding

oh i'm sure
it would take some getting used to
walking backward that way
things constantly flying into my hands
but if i could start at the end
and put death behind me
at the beginning
just think of that!

going to sleep each night
waking up a little younger
mind clearing
strength returning
able to thread a needle
and throw a fast-ball again

and desire
stirring like a summer breeze
the flag barely moving at first
then flying triumphant
in the prevailing wind

as the days lengthen however
i realize
i am trading away lived experience
for adolescent energy
and a full head of hair

suddenly
my father comes back to life

and once again
i take him for granted
i begin to shrink
until sinking to my knees
i roll over in my crib
and wave "good-bye" to my feet

stripped of all identity
toothless and bald again
i slip back inside my mother
to dissolve in the darkness
of absolute non-being

2.

THEY ARE ALL GONE NOW
AND SO ARE YOU

ON HIGHWAY 1

there were
young men with long hair
bare-foot girls
and big black dogs
wearing red bandannas
once upon a time
there were
but...
they are all gone now
and so are you

standing in front of the bank
behind a gleaming line
of brand-new refrigerators
pitching EST

i liked you better
in Big Sur
on smokey wine-soaked afternoons
depressed

with rotten teeth

SANCTUARY

at the clinic
it was standing-room only
the patients caught up in *Time*
lost in *Life*
the lucky ones
fighting in the Middle East
and reviewing the latest movies
once removed
from the grim receptionist
who called out our names
one by one like death

and i
a candidate for a Root Canal
with nothing left in the magazine rack
but *House Beautiful*
and a dozen copies of *Dental Digest*

well you do what you can
with what you have
and pictured on page 54
was a bare room
completely unfurnished
except for a bright green air-fern
hanging beside
an enormous
stark white
rattan chair

and it was there
that i sat
with my legs crossed
glaring at the man
who had *The New Yorker*

ALFRED E. NEUMAN
AND THE BRAVE NEW WORLD

consider
coming out of the cave
entering a Prehistoric World
teaming with saber-toothed tigers
our primal ancestors
on Librium

"what me worry?"

imagine
Leo Buscaglia
"Mr. Love...Mr. Hug"
practicing what he preaches
at the time of the Black Plague

not at all sure
how much better off we are
i remain
   as anxious
   and antisocial
   as ever
the
lone survivor

WATER SPOTS

yes
even Sergeant York
missed occasionally

and i'm told
by certain female intimates
that all across the civilized world
women have moped—muttering
if the target is that hard to hit
why can't a man making his stand
just sit?

however women
a musketeer's aim and marksmanship
are not the problem here
as in the game of darts
dead center is not
where the big points are scored
it's the half inch of

** silence **

at the edge of the pond
the thin strip of porcelain
and flirting this way with the rim
even an expert can't be expected
to keep all of his darts on the board

i don't know who made up the rules
or why
but for some reason prudence
prefers the hush of the hard surface
to the voice of the laughing pool

which makes no sense at all men
considering the symphony we go through
whistling and coughing
and clearing our throats
when intruders approach in the hall
why not simply
let 'em know we're in there
with the sweet sound of a waterfall?

now there's a liberating thought!

from this day forward
i shall let the work speak for itself
and by so doing
show some real concern for the clean-up-crew
killing two birds with one stone
my sights as well as my consciousness raised

i for one
will blaze away at the bulls-eye
a welcome visitor
known by women the world over
as a straight shooter

A LARGELY INHERITED
AND UNALTERABLE TENDENCY
TO DESIRE SILENCE

in sand
on pine needles
a man can keep his vow of silence
but not in a modern convenience
flooded to the rim
with no shoreline
to go upon in quiet meditation

how humiliating!
to stand before God
and everyone else within earshot
announcing one's imperfection

acoustically
giving our position away
spooking the game
putting the enemy on alert
instinctual no-no's
i'd say

and yet like a wolf
trotting from house to house
the civilized male is obliged
to mark off his territory
in disinfected pails of water

is it any wonder then
that modern men these days
under pressure
are melting into the shadows
and losing themselves in the trees

PULLING A TIGER'S TEETH

whenever you feel
like saying:
           what did i do?
try saying:
           how can i help?

BOOMERANG

"do you know what they call
a boomerang
that doesn't return?

a stick!"

and though
she is a wonderfully talented
and creative woman
my wife simply cannot repeat a joke

"do you know what they call
a boomerang
that doesn't return?

a piece of wood!"

accurate
as those early scholars
who first transcribed the living word
but missed the cosmic joke

"I Command You
To Love Me
Of Your Own Free Will!"

a boomerang
i'd say—

AMERICA CHECKS OUT
OF THE HOTEL DE SADE

the Greeks had Zeus
and Hera
Hestia and Hermes
to explain away the mystery

that was
until the Age of Reason
transformed them into myth
and superstition

and now
just when Pharmacist
and Physician
have most of the social diseases
on the run

when birth control
has advanced to the place
where a starved populace
can finally fool around
and have a little fun

down from Olympus
like a thunderbolt
to a lightning-rod
leaping
into the national conscience
from a cover story
in *Time* magazine
comes Herpeeees!

and you say there's no God

THE FIRST LADY

on a popular television game show
a man and woman co-host
they appear together
while he runs down the list of prizes

    the exciting self-supporting
    medium-duty jib crane
    with pillar-base mounting!

    a year's supply of Carter's
    non-wrinkling waterproof rubber cement
    for problem-free paper sticking!

and of course the biggie!

    the all-expense paid
    weekend vacation
    on the island of Guam!

as always
trying to make something out of nothing
i study the face of the female
on camera
but not speaking
the enthusiastic listener
who eagerly nods over each item
emitting little testimonial sounds
from a tiny round mouth

    ooh! ah! oh!

cringing
i wonder what it would take
to have me standing at someone's elbow

like that
            animated
            with my arms dangling

the audience
loving me for it

THE SOAPS

taking a nap
with my eyes open
i watch
not really caring what happens

because they are there
i say
the *Days of Our Lives*
there blocking the afternoon sun

if only the murder were solved
the pardon granted
if only Doug would drop the gun
and go back to bed with Julie

the loose ends all tied up on Friday
on Monday
there's no telling who
might return from the dead

or
as in the case
of a lonely old woman i know
vice versa

OLD ORAIBI
AND THE VIDEO-PHONE

imagine looking into the eyes
of the voice speaking in your ear
putting substance with sound
imagine the improvement
in interpersonal communication

when a poet speaks near Old Oraibi
the Native Americans
hear everything that is said
while watching the ceiling and floor

> "...never the face
> it would be a display
> of disrespect
> to intrude in such a private place
>
> we only stare at those
> who are not quite human beings
> for furniture salesmen
> and government agents
> we have a saying:
>
> do not step sideways too quickly
> white-eyes
> or you will surely disappear"

as she spoke
the Hopi woman smiled
studying the sky

elsewhere
the advent of the video-phone
will turn out to be
little more
than a boon for flashers

MURRAY STORIES

on the eve
of his military induction
half-swacked
a bunch of us took Murray
out to where Fast Francis lived
cracking up
as he thrashed in the ivy
climbing to her second-story window

"go away Murray
   you're drunk!"

and laughing madly
shouting Batmaaaannnnnnnnn!
he launched himself out
into the night
a short flight that ended badly
on the business end of a garden spigot

"gored
   by a rampaging Rainbird!" he whooped
as an unamused
Emergency Ward doctor attempted to close
the foolish grin in his scrotum

at dawn
we passed the jug around
said our "good-byes"
and watched him board the Greyhound
gingerly keeping his legs
in the exact shape of a croquet-hoop

next afternoon
he was waiting for us

at the Cork & Bottle
out on a short medical deferment
a length of time that became
the celebration
none of us remembered anything about

oh
the tales we love to tell!

a close friend
even going to the trouble
of building a small redwood deck
off his living room
a place he claims
created specifically for the two of us
to drink
and tell our Murray stories on

yesterday
somewhat wistfully he mentioned
that the space has not been used
since i began recovering

A NEGATIVE PEACE

out of the tenderloin
the madman came
a length of twine trailing from one hand
doing the breast stroke with the other

"clear the way!
  clear the way!
  here comes my submarine!"

the crowd separated
and spread-eagled against the buildings
one by one
they sank into the stone

"submarine!
  submarine!
  step aside for my submarine!"

cars skidded and turned over
traffic snarled
and when he saw i wasn't buying it
he screamed

"LOOK OUT!
  RADIOACTIVE WAR MACHINE!"

right here
the question surfaces—
should i back off and give him more reason
to believe he has what he thinks he has
on the end of that string?

or should i stubbornly stand my ground
refusing to budge
and risk getting myself
run down by the damn thing?

42

A VERY SERIOUS ARTIST

when he wasn't teaching art
at the Community College
he was in his studio
making rocks out of store-bought clay

small stones
pebbles—pieces of gravel
buckets and buckets full
modeled after specimens
collected earlier
in a previous life

no question about it
in a natural setting
his creations were convincing enough
to fool even an expert

rumor has it
he once lived somewhere
other than Odessa Texas
by the sea they say
with a woman

some of us it would seem
stubbornly try to recall feelings
when all we can really do
is remember we had them

A PHILOSOPHER

for Bob O'Brian

an honest-to-God Philosopher
lives in the mountains close to me
farther up though
and much farther back

he is
the Department at a local College
eighty miles round trip each day
he goes the distance for questions

twice now
he has summoned me personally
to help him with a problem
he couldn't handle by himself

1. a twenty-four-foot house trailer
   down a sixty-percent slope
   we almost lost it
   on the dogleg left

2. a ton of machinery
   over a precipice on a frayed rope
   was the only way
   to get the pump to water

twice now we have seen the strawberry
growing on the face of the cliff
twice now
we have almost eaten it

it would seem then
that a Philosopher by definition
is someone who has dedicated his life
to putting heavy things in hard places

44

REMEMBERING ALAN

i've been told
that the church won't saint a man
until he's been dead
at least fifty years
and that's too bad
for who will be around then
to tell us how he talked too much
and used to pick his nose

let me tell about a saint of mine
who
not so long ago
was alive and well and living
in California

i had read every word he had written
and could recite his punch lines
like the rosary
he was only a writer of books then
though

he became a saint the night we met
and he was drunk
and fell on the floor vomiting
and.....

set me free

STRINGS ATTACHED

i have given gifts
trinkets
inexpensive tokens of my affection
but with instructions
that you must pass them along
give them away
to someone you love and admire

and when you do
i am crushed

HOPE-GIVE IT UP!

i hope
i continue to look like Cary Grant
blessed
with this marvelous shock of hair!

i hope
my marital relationship
continues to change and grow
the way i think it should

i hope
my kids turn out alright
that is
according to my idea of alright

i hope
i don't have to die—today
but if i do
i hope i don't embarrass myself

i hope
there is life after death
and if there is
i hope i don't have to remember this one

hope—
give it up!
and begin to trust the process

3.

NOTES FROM A TROUBADOUR
AND TRAVELING SALESMAN

IN THE CONCOURSE OF MY LIFE

some airports
teem with ugly people
men in sweat-soaked shirts
women with caked make-up
lips the color of dirt
human sacks of potatoes
passing through the security device

some airports
gleam with shining faces
stylish commuters
wholesome as yogurt
Swiss yodelers yodeling
lovers running—laughing
holding hands at the baggage carousel

glum and glowering
bright and glowing
it entirely depends
upon my own comings and goings

TRAVELS
WITH THE WAGON MASTER
AND A SANITARY ENGINEER

i am a straight-forward
goal-oriented
linear-type traveler
vacationing
like Patton racing for the Rhine

the unsmiling map-in-the-lap
mile-a-minute kind
in touch with where we are
where we're going
constantly
updating the arrival time

right on schedule
yet plagued by the dreadful thought
that at any moment
my wife will wake from her nap
open her eyes
and see the road sign that says

HISTORICAL MARKER
2 Miles Ahead

and she
on the road
becomes a devout sanitarian
scouring the countryside
both figuratively and literally

opening motel doors
with curled lip
and Lysol spray can going

"if you plan to sleep with me
  tonight

52

keep your feet off this filthy floor!"

at bedtime
throwing back the covers
surveying the linen landscape
praying
that this time
there will be no sign
no

    historical marker
    of another kind

THE POTLUCK CIRCUIT

a tossed salad
lost in a field of tossed salads
i try to distinguish myself
by describing the flavor of tarragon
with gestures
i long to be experienced

like Langston Hughes
i too have wilted
watching a house erode
between the potluck
and the poetry reading

"we'd love to stay
but we really must go
the ostriches you know..."

and it's just as indigestible
at the head table
where the fancy covered dishes
congregate

"look out for this one Sidney
it has liver in it..."

everyone sneaking a peek
to see what a poet looks like
eating cole-slaw
marveling
at how smoothly his jaw moves

staring straight ahead
i ask myself why
just being at the table
has never been enough

THE POET ADDRESSES
THE WESTERN UNITED STATES
REGIONAL CONFERENCE
OF AIRPORT MANAGERS
AND THEIR WIVES

when i arrived the microphone and stool
said: Barry Manilow
when they should have been saying:
Robert Bly

the chairman of the program committee
suggesting
that if i would also play guitar during dinner
there'd be an extra fifty in it for me

to which i responded
with a quick thumb-nail sketch
of Vachel Lindsay

later
after the welcome
the awards
and the election of new officers
i was tendered to an audience
filled with Tony Bennett expectations

and for thirty intoxicating minutes
i was the only person
on the face of the earth
who knew
what was coming next

BY ANY OTHER NAME

most of us
it would seem
are trying to live up to
or struggling to rise above
the momentary whimsy
of our parents

and what could mine
have been thinking of
calling me Ricky?
Rickys never amount to anything
Hamiltons
address joint sessions of Congress
Sterlings race Maseratis
but Ricky?
hell
it's lucky i didn't grow up to be
a German Shepard

and i've recently noted
that the Ricks
who drop the k for theatrical reasons
have become the groundlings
of the movie industry
never credited as writer
director or star
bestboy and gaffer is what we are
boomman and grip
shunned
by women of mystery and elegance
Ric goes home with Patty or Babs

oh to have been cristened
Wallace or Gregory

taken seriously
by editors of literary quarterlies
the Sidneys and Sheldons
who never venture beyond my name
convinced
that anything composed by a Ric
would have to be Mother's Day drivel
or doggerel for girlie magazines

desperate
i toy with the idea of running
first and last name together
ignoring the space
as children often do
becoming Ricmasten
taking the lotus position
like Krishnamurti
venerated at last
but impossible
to find in the phone book

THE THIRTY-YEAR
CLASS REUNION

chatting with the Astronauts
on the White House lawn
addressing a brace of Eagle Scouts
Mr. President
are you aware that your face
is on a dart-board
the eyes punched out

    and years later
    when only the winners
    would remember
    what was said about them
    in the high school yearbook
    i'm told of a game
    my classmates played
    whenever i left the room

    even at this late date
    i'm shocked to think of myself
    as an amusing pastime
    something one did in study hall
    and in the cafeteria
    something
    to laugh about now
    with a bunch of elderly adolescents
    suddenly gone sour

    how could i have been
    so oblivious
    so out of touch
    with what must have been written
    all over their faces

    "The Kick Ric Game"!

a collector's item
Mr. President
a keepsake
for your Library no doubt

having nothing at all
to do
with your re-election

A POET?

being published
means something only
on the date of publication

had i known this
i would never have listed my occupation
as "Poet"
when filling out forms
at the Credit Union

i would have been
better off
had i described myself
as voyeur
or manic-depressive

i can see now
i should have slept on it
accomplishments never seem to survive
a good night's sleep

the rejection slips however
the dead ends
are always there in the morning
like that bully-kid
who gave me such a hard time
on the way to school

sneering
asking me again today
what it is
that i really do for a living

READY TO BE PAPERED

as a boy
i could never bring myself
to close my wooden birds
the ribs were always left exposed
the balsa framework never knew
the feel of paper skin

"i think they look better that way"
 i'd say
 the truth was
 i could never keep the tissue
 from wrinkling

and if nothing ever flew
nothing failed either

today
i tinker with words
and delight in trying my ideas out
on every passer-by
i fly the outlines
tell the punch lines
describing in detail
the prize-winners i am about to write

as before
i keep myself surrounded
by the superstructure
of slowly turning dreams

and still it seems
nothing
really in the sky

STATISTICS SAY

statistics say:

—that each day in America
   there is more violent crime perpetrated
   than books of poetry purchased

—that in any given period of time
   the incidence of child abuse
   will exceed the number of poems composed

in this great country of ours
the odds of someone becoming a bard
are a hundred times less
than that
of being blinded by an exploding pop-bottle

and if the figures are correct
i think we can say
without fear of contradiction
that here in the United States
the poetry problem
is clearly under control

WITH SICK FRIENDS

this time
the pencils have all gone dull
and listless

the typewriter
prattles
like a fever-ridden child

pad and paper
stare vacantly
the eyes of imbeciles

at my writing desk
i sit with the invalid
tools of my trade

looking
for signs of improvement
i fear the worst

FOR THE ENTRANTS
OF THE MISSISSIPPI JR. COLLEGE
CREATIVE WRITING CONTEST

it being the South
the expectation was
that some unborn Capote
would leap from the competition
and take me by the throat
or
that i would find myself
forgiving
an adolescent Kathryn Ann Porter
for being a bit sophomoric
my picky criticism
punctured
by at least one poignant phrase

the reluctant judge
amazed in the end
and delivered
by a painfully green
yet promising James Dickey

alas
this was not to be
for either
i have gone blind
(always a possibility)
or
the needle in the haystack
simply wasn't there to find

in any case
i can only wonder now
would it have been easier
to pick an ace
from a pack of aces?

tomorrow
some latent William Faulkner
may emerge from all of this
and prove me wrong
but not sorry
a critic is never sorry
for
if you let my red pen
turn you from your love of language
to a desolate and dreary life
pumping gas
          that then
          is where you belong

ON THE BEST-SELLER LIST
AND ONLY THREE PAGES LONG

Chapter One.   On first meeting
                    reject them totally

Chapter Two.   The next time around,
                    be halfway civil.

Chapter Three.   Now let yourself
                    be completely captivated.

it's true
the world does not need
another *How-To-Book*
but if i were to write one
i would title it:

> *How to Make Friends*
> *With Important People*

and i would dedicate it
to you

TRYING IS
NOT GOOD ENOUGH

i'm trying
not to write this poem
trying not to be clever and snide
about the tourists with whom i ate
in a Howard Johnsons
halfway across the state of Kansas

i'm trying
to be more tolerant these days
even of overweight women
who dress in polyester
and of tall skinny men
in red Caterpillar caps

God knows!.....i'm trying!
but sometimes
a poem writes itself

BACKSTAGE

i am often taken in
by the stage-craft pictured
on the pages of *Sunset* magazine
settings
that speak to me somehow
saying:

> in this breakfast nook
> you will never be lonely again

and i should know better
i who reside in a theatrical set
propped up on the apron
of the Santa Lucia mountains

from the road
everything looks real enough
but i know the walls
are made of painted rags
and the tower
sways in the slightest breeze

on Sundays
they stream out from the city
passenger cars creeping by
people pointing
living for a moment in a poet's dream

i wave from the window
why not?
how could they know there's nothing
behind any of this
nothing except
what they bring to it themselves

this is not to say
that in this living space
there are not those rare moments
when we gather on the deck
to see a crescent moon at sunset
the air alive
with the sound of Rainbirds
whispering down in the garden

but
in the theater
when the audience goes home
there is always that
one unblinking naked lightbulb
left on backstage

A TROUBADOUR
& TRAVELING SALESMAN

at home
my heart is a wristwatch
and there is always a dog
in the calendar

suddenly i am a rabbit
breaking cover
my ears up in the wind
i go sailing

the mountains
drain from my window
underfoot the floor moves
the waiting is over

outward bound
we clear the harbor
like farmers
coming in from the field

4.

SEVEN SONGS
UNSUNG

A MATTER OF TIME

This is a matter of time
and a busted watch on a chain.
A matter of time,
And missing my plane.
I'm half the way 'round,
With halfway yet to go
And this old broken watch
Is running too slow.

Now, the jewelers
Have all kinds of time in a case.
Some so unlikely
I couldn't find the face.
And they're selling me one
That won't hardly wind,
When I need a watch
That keeps better time.

Cause if I miss the plane,
It will leave me behind.
And life is a game
I must re-define.
But finding oneself
Is such a hard thing to find
When everyone's watch
Keeps different time.

And everyone's watch
keeps different time.

DOWN IN THE KITCHEN

You rise up in the morning
With things not seeming right.
You've lost the easy feelin'
You were feelin' late last night.
So you wander into the kitchen
and stand there tryin' to think.
Searchin' for some meaning
Down the kitchen sink.

I know, I know,
I've been there too,
I've been down in the kitchen
Same as you.

You go through all the cupboards
And check the Frigidaire.
You don't know what you're hungry for
But you're sure it isn't there.
And you can't find all the pieces
For the coffee-pot,
So you sit down at the table
And read the Cornflakes box.

I know, I know.
I've been there too,
I've been down in the kitchen
Same as you.

You gaze out of the window
As you sit there killin' time.
Fingering the milk you spilled
Out into a design.
You drop a piece of silverware
But you leave it where it lies

And stare at the linoleum
Makin' patterns with your eyes

I know, I know.
I've been there too.
I've been down in the kitchen
Same as you.

Now the streets are full of people
Who seem to have it made,
But we've all been down in the kitchen
Lonely and afraid.
So wash your dirty dishes
And put away your glass,
And go out from the kitchen
As though you've been to Mass.

Go out from your kitchen
and know you've been to Mass.

BARBIE DOLL

A slender little waist.
A pretty little face.
That's Barbie with every hair in place
There's no rebellion in a Barbie Doll
There's just a little empty space.

Barbie Doll, Barbie Doll.
Oh, what a perfect world
This world would be
If every little girl were a Barbie!

She loves to look her best
In a new expensive dress.
For Barbie this is happiness.
Invest your money in a Barbie Doll,
She's not the kind to protest.

Chorus.

When she sees something new
Made of taffeta and blue
Your Barbie has got to have one too
And all the Bankers must love Barbie Doll
'Cause they're glad to loan the money to you.

Chorus.

She sees a lot of Ken
Ah, but he is just a friend.
And Barbie she'll not give in to him.
You've got no problems with your Barbie Dolls,
'Cause you can't tell her from him.

Chorus.

There's not a bit of strife
With a Barbie in your life
With a Barbie for a daughter or a wife.
No, there's not one problem in a Barbie Doll,
And also not a bit of life.

Chorus.

FRED THE FIRST
AND AMAZING GRACE

Fred was the best dog we ever had,
Even though he was with us
Only thirty-three days.
I believe it was on Good Friday
That Fred ran off with the Hippies.
And at times,
We still think we see him
Riding in the front-seat of old VWs,
Looking down the road seriously.

And Fred was the only dog
We ever had
That would fetch a stick.
It didn't matter that someone else
Taught him this trick,
As I've said, Fred
Was the best dog we ever had,
Even though he was with us only thirty-three days,
And I suppose that's the reason why.

We have Grace now.
Amazing Grace!
Who wets on my foot,
Chews up my valuables,
Bit my best friend!
We've had her five long years,
And she will be with us until she dies.
Fred was the best dog we ever had!
But you know? We really do love
That Amazing Grace.

WINDOWS

All night long the rain came down.
Left water standing all around.
Muddy puddles on the ground,
Reflect the morning sky.

Windows, windows,
Look through those windows.
Windows, windows,
Look into my eyes.

Down the road there came a man
He was walking on his hands,
And no one seemed to understand.
No one even tries to.

And everywhere the stranger goes,
People put their chairs in rows.
They sit and listen to his clothes
And no one hears him crying—

Windows!

Upside-down he walks the street.
His mental breakdown was complete
Cause when they said: "Stand on your feet!"
He would ask them: "Why?"

He came by the other day.
His quiet eyes did seem to say:
"I will journey all the way,
   Out to your horizons."

All night long the rain came down.
Left water standing all around.
Muddy puddles on the ground,
Reflect the morning sky.

PALOMINO

While ridin' the ridgeline above the Big Sur
In the barranca I saw somethin' stir.
A wild golden stallion with a mane white as snow
And I swore I'd corral me that palomino.

I tried hard to catch him for forty-nine days,
But I was outwitted in forty-nine ways.
Then up an arroyo I gets him boxed in.
And when I'd lassoed him the fight did begin.

Palomino, palomino
I swore I'd corral me that palomino.

The strain on my saddle, it made the cinch bust,
That crazy hoss drags me a mile through the dust.
Then he pulls up real sudden and wheelin' around,
He comes back to stomp me right into the ground.

Well I took off a runnin' and went up a tree.
He circls below like he's laughin' at me.
But the rope I'd put on him was trailin' behind,
And in one of the branches it soon was entwined.

Palomino, palomino,
I swore I'd corral me that palomino.

He fought like a demon but the rope, it held fast.
And I said: "Palomino, I got you at last!"
He bucked for an hour, then he fell on his side,
And I knew he was mine when the hobbles were tied.

I set down plum tuckered and rolled me a smoke.
Studied the brave hoss that I had just broke,
He knew he was beaten, He'd lost all his fight,
And deep down inside me this didn't seem right.

Palomino, palomino
I swore I'd corral me that palomino.

And then in an instant I knew what to do.
I pulled off the hobbles and cut the lasso.
He stood there a moment, just lookin' at me,
Like he's tryin' to thank me for settin' him free.

One slap on his flank and away he did fly.
And watchin' him vanish I starts in to cry.
Wherever I wander. Wherever I go,
My heart is still back with that palomino.

Palomino, palomino.
My heart is still back with that palomino.

KITES AND LAKES

I stood at the foot of the ladder.
I thought I wanted to climb.
I spat in my hand,
And called to the man
Who sat at the top at the time.
Said: "Sir, I'm just a beginner,
Who wants to scale those heights.
Will you give me a hand:"
And that beautiful man said:
"Go fly a kite!"

So I went down to the hardware store.
And bought me a ball of string.
Found some pretty paper there,
Some sticks and everything.

Then I sat down on the kitchen floor
With my sticks and string and glue.
I was older than I used to be,
But I still knew what to do.

Then I went up on a windy hill
To join the children there.
They came to help me put my kite
High up in the air.

I look over my shoulder now,
And now the breezes rise.
I start to run and wonder of wonders
She flies! See how she flies!

And so good advice was given.
The beautiful man was right.
Cause you ain't really livin'
Till you go fly a kite.

I watched them follow the leader.
And pass in their plastic parade.
I fell in line,
Fell in behind
The folks who all had it made.
I said: "People, I'm a believer,
Who sorely needs a break."
And the boys up ahead
Smiled as they said:
"Go jump in the lake!"

So I went out to the countryside
And found a little stream.
It led me down a canyon deep,
Then across a meadow green.

I went where the water went
And took each turn it made
It led me to a quiet lake
In the weeping willow shade.

I went out on that grassy bank
And stripped down to my skin.
While all the little children there
Called me to come in.

I stand above the water now,
High on a mossy stump.
I hold my nose, and shout: Here goes!
And I jump. See how I jump.

So when good advice is given,
That's the kind to take.
Cause you ain't really livin'
Till you jump in the lake.

83

BACKWORD

REV. RIC
AND "THAT OLD TIME" KARMA

There aren't many old time travelling preachers on the road these days, but a few have survived past the " Electronic Age" and carry on an art form which, though dying, lives on here and there in the backwaters of America. Among this paltry army of snake-oil and salvation salesmen is one Ric Masten who alone in the brotherhood is pushing the gospel of karma. Karma? Gospel? And you thought karma was the universal *law* of cause and effect. Yet Ric has found a way to market even karma to unsuspecting students, housewives, and prisoners across the country without ever mentioning it. The artistry of Rev. Ric's performance is a thing of beauty, for the listener never has the slightest idea that he or she is being brainwashed by Dr. Tao into the great eastern mysteries. This neo-Hindu apostle has well perfected his transliteration of the *Upanishads* doctrines to an American audience through the clever guise of an itinerant poet. He has turned a law into a gospel by preaching the virtues of what is sometimes referred to as "good karma". "Tell somebody today that you love them," says this bandwagon bodhisattva to yet another flock of fledgling fadists. Yet, the illusion is never discovered. Ric's hidden career as the guru of good karma never comes to light. School administrators and English department chairmen are only *too* happy to hire an "established" poet to come into their classrooms for a few hours to give their students a

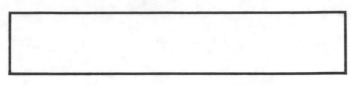

little "culture" (so long as they don't have to listen), never realizing that the culture they are giving their students is "eastern culture".

And so here comes evangelist Ric, on the skin of it as American as acne, spreading karma like so much seed corn and hoping some of it will take root after he is gone. Working his audience with an ear sublimely tuned to the slightest nuances of reaction and waiting for the smallest chuckle or inaudible sigh to believe that the message might be getting through. To capture his listeners, this Alan Watts avatar loads his talks with a veritable *NATIONAL ENQUIRER* of human interest poems and stories which are used as the occasion demands. Ric endlessly searches for the right theme to convey his message of karma love. And then, finally, the audiences do respond, for they know instinctively there is truth in this zen master's koans. And, there are those moments of pure satori when students say that he has helped them unlock their inner selfscape.

The day of the travelling preacher is past, but luckily Rev. Ric hasn't heard the word yet and goes right on bringing his light from the east.

Paul Benson
Mountain View College
Dallas, Texas

BOOKS

Also available on order, through local bookstores that use R. R. Bowker Company BOOKS IN PRINT catalogue system

☐ THEY ARE ALL GONE NOW
   . . .And So Are YOU by Ric Masten   **Paperback $6.00**
   106 pages. ISBN 0-931104-15-7

☐ EVEN AS WE SPEAK by Ric Masten.   **Paperback $5.50**
   112 pages. ISBN 0-931104-12-2

☐ the DESERTED ROOSTER by Ric Masten.   **Paperback $5.00**
   96 pages. ISBN 0-931104-11-4

☐ STARK NAKED by Ric Masten.   ☐ **Paperback $5.00**
   110 pages. ISBN 0-931104-04-1   ☐ **Hardcover $10.00**

☐ VOICE OF THE HIVE by Ric Masten.   **Paperback $5.00**
   104 pages. ISBN 0-931104-02-5

☐ DRAGONFLIES, CODFISH & FROGS by Ric Masten.   **Paperback $5.50**
   112 pages. ISBN 0-931104-06-8

☐ HIS & HERS by Ric & Billie Masten.   **Paperback $5.00**
   80 pages. ISBN 0-931104-01-7

☐ BILLIE BEETHOVEN   **Paperback $5.00**
   by Billie Barbara Masten.
   96 pages. ISBN 0-931104-13-0

TAPES

☐ Ric Masten Singing
   LET IT BE A DANCE   **Price $5.95**
   12 Songs. Stereo SF-1002

BROADSIDES . . . Price $1.00

Single sheets printed on colored stock. 8½"x11", suitable for framing.

☐ The Warty Frog   ☐ Let It Be a Dance
☐ The Second Half   ☐ The Homesick Snail
☐ Water Spots

PUBLICITY PAMPHLETS

☐ Ric Masten in Concert . . . ☐ On the College Campus.
☐ In the High School . . . ☐ In the Middle School.
☐ In the Elementary . . . ☐ In the Church . . . ☐ On Relationships.
☐ Honorarium and Fee Schedule.

CHECKS MADE OUT TO

SUNFLOWER INK
Palo Colorado Canyon
Carmel, CA 93923

               ORDER $ _____

    6% SALES TAX (CA. RES.)   _____

    SHIPPING & HANDLING $ __$1.25___

              TOTAL $ _____

Name _____

Address _____

City _____ State _____ Zip _____